.30 M1 GARAND

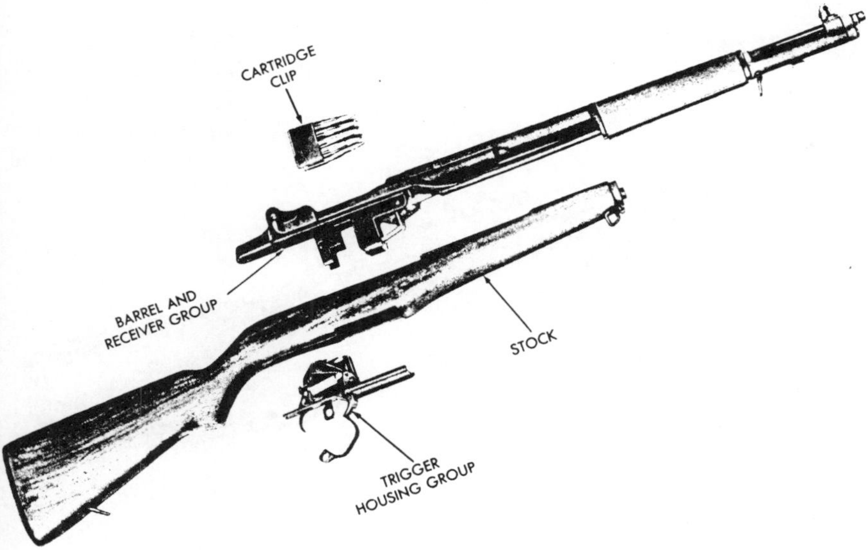
CARTRIDGE CLIP
BARREL AND RECEIVER GROUP
STOCK
TRIGGER HOUSING GROUP

Top to bottom—
Rifle U.S. Cal. .30, M1,
right & left views.
Rifle U.S. Cal. .30, M1C
Rifle U.S. Cal. .30, M1D

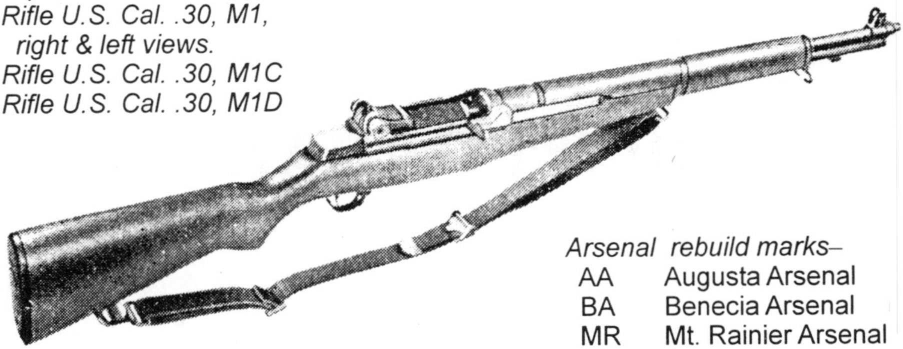

Arsenal rebuild marks–

AA	Augusta Arsenal
BA	Benecia Arsenal
MR	Mt. Rainier Arsenal
RA	Raritan Arsenal
RRA	Red River Arsenal
RIA	Rock Island Arsenal
SA	Springfield Arsenal

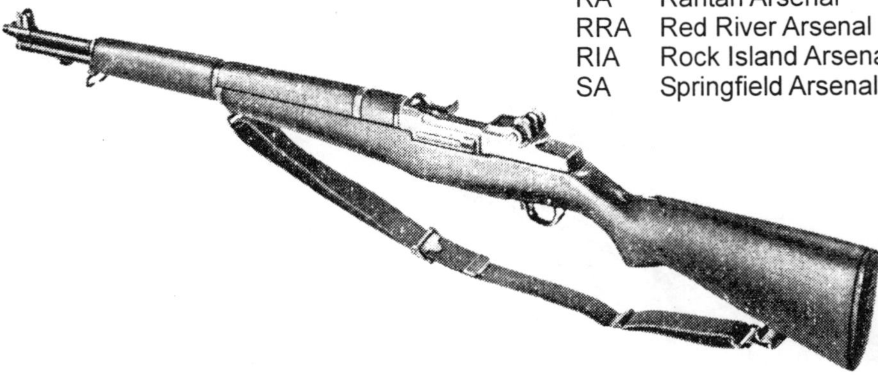

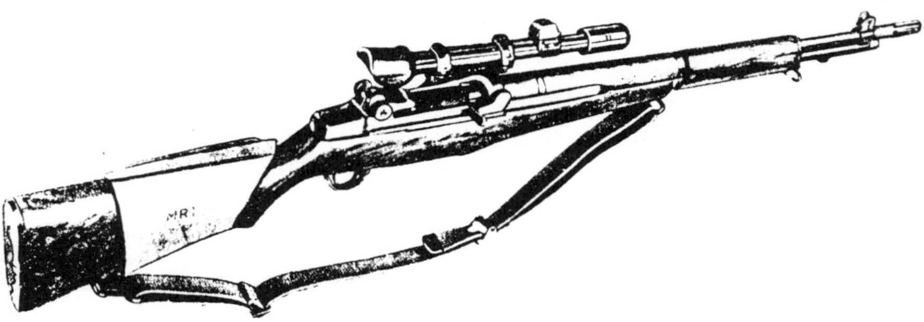

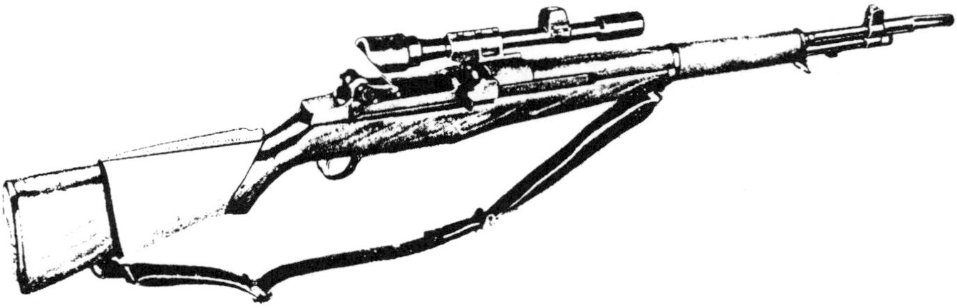

IDENTIFICATION ...

The U.S. M1 Garand is readily recognized, the rifle designation, maker and rifle serial number are marked on the top of the action, on the flat area behind the aperture sight. During its service life through World War 2 and the Korean War as the regulation issue for army, navy, marines and air force personnel, the lack of substantial changes make the M1 Garand unique in comparison with its contempories in service with other countries at the time.

Purist M1 Garand collectors note the production, contractor, code and parts number markings and dates such as are found on the barrel, along with manufacturing differences, all of which may seem routine to the average eye. The protective finish to metal and wood along with the cartouche stock marks, can often indicate the service life and arsenal repair or refits applied to a specific rifle.

Such differences can also reveal various service and surplus parts replacements; many collectors prefer their pieces to be as original as possible, as first issued or used in any particular theatre. Other enthusiasts however are more interested in a reliable shooter or a finely tuned competition match rifle; all owners look for different features in their particular rifles.

In-house Garand development saw 'E' suffix model designations, M1E1 through M1E12 and test rifles with a 'T' prefix allocated, particularly T20 through T44 which served as a 7.62mm M14 prototype. Such development however is more the domain of avid and dedicated collectors, outside our scope here.

Sniper models were introduced into service in 1944, the M1C with telescope mounted offset on the action, and M1D with its scope mounted at the rear of the barrel. Various telescopic sights were used on these rifles. Lyman Alaskan and Griffin & Howe variants were designated as M73, M82, M83 and M84 sights on the M1.

As a match rifle, the .30 M1 Garand saw few equals. National Match models were set up at Springfield Armory from 1953. After 1959, up until 1963, only the rebuilt N.M. models were set up at Springfield. Early rifles were new built, others were reworks of prior National Match models. Such rifles were stamped 'NM' on specific components such as the barrel muzzle and backsight parts. A hooded fine adjustment backsight and glass bedded stock also became available on the National Match rifles.

The M1 bayonet evolved through the 16.2-in. long blade 'M1942' or earlier M1905 usually with black composition grips (interchangeable on the Mod. 1903 Springfield) and its M3 or M10 scabbard, the M1 model with 10-in. blade and cut-down M1905E1 counterpart both with the shorter M7 scabbard.

The M5A1 bayonet of the late 1950's had a new locking system, a spear point blade and dimpled plastic grips, it was issued with the M8A1 scabbard as used on other models with similar blades. The M1905, M1942, M1 and M1905E1 bayonets feature a muzzle ring while the M5A1 bayonet has a shorter crossguard with 7mm stud which fixes into the gas plug recess and only fits the M1 rifle.

Other service accessories include sling, cleaning gear, winter trigger, grenade launcher and sight with flash hider and leather cheek rest options for the telescope-mounter sniper variants.

Specific collector and user references are listed at the end of this handbook, there are also various websites and forums which cater specifically for the M1 Garand; newcomers are usually welcome and detailed information shared. Surplus parts dealers in the United States are a good source for replacement parts and accessories too, regular advertising in Shotgun News and Gun List magazines.

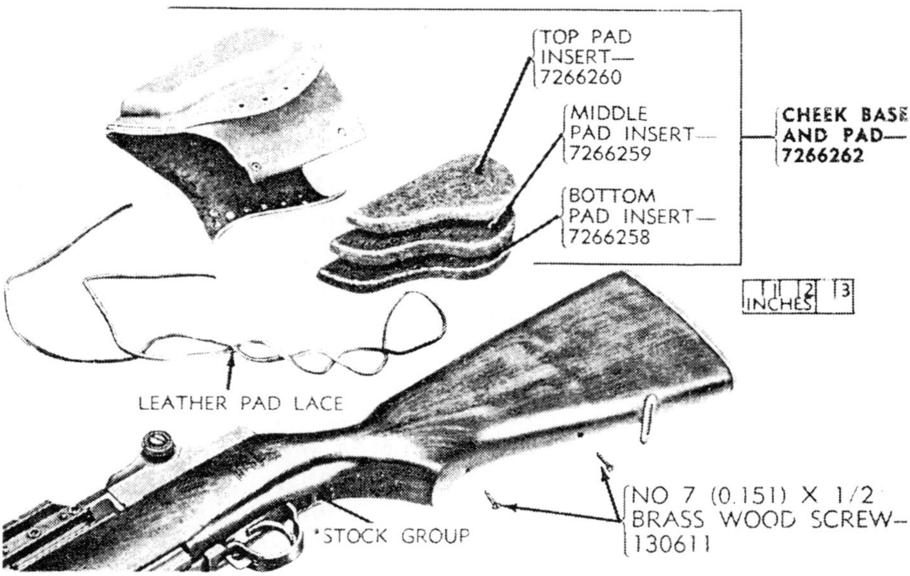

Sniper model .30 M1C Garand with cheek piece fittings

STRIPPING ...

REMOVAL of the THREE MAIN GROUPS ...

Barrel & Receiver Group
Trigger Housing Group
Stock Group

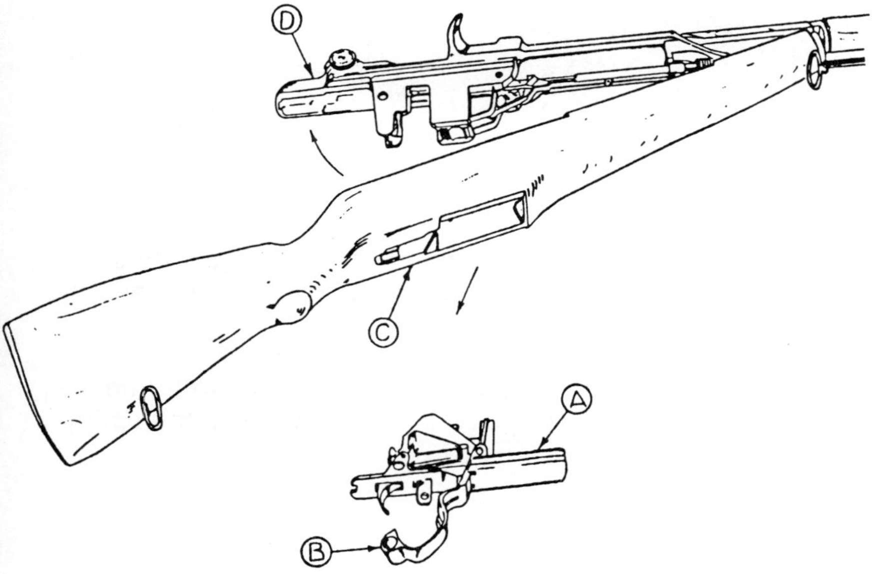

1. Unlock the trigger housing group (A) by pulling the trigger guard (B) to the rear to disengage its clip, and then pull the trigger guard downwards to unlock the trigger housing group from the receiver.

2. Remove the trigger housing group (A) by grasping the trigger guard (B) and pull outward from stock.

3. Separate the barrel and receiver group (D) from the stock (C) by pulling them apart.

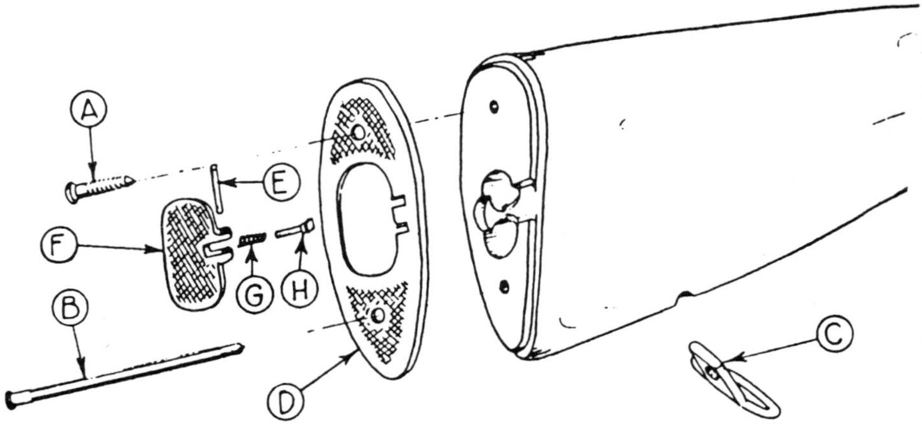

4. Unscrew the small butt plate screw (A) and long plate screw (B). The swivel (C) and butt plate (D) can now be removed.

5. To dismantle the butt plate (D), punch out cap pin (E) and remove the plate cap (F). The butt plate plunger (H) and spring (G) can now be removed.

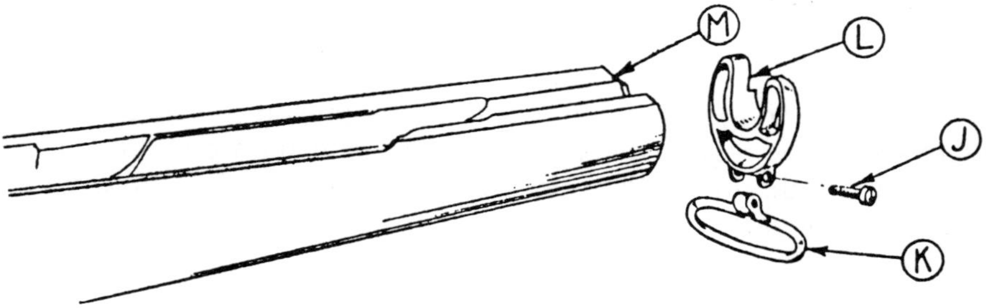

6. Unscrew the stock ferrule screw (J) and remove the stock swivel (K) from the stock ferrule (L) and tap off the ferrule (L) from the stock (M).

REMOVAL OF GAS CYLINDER GROUP and FRONT HAND GUARD ...

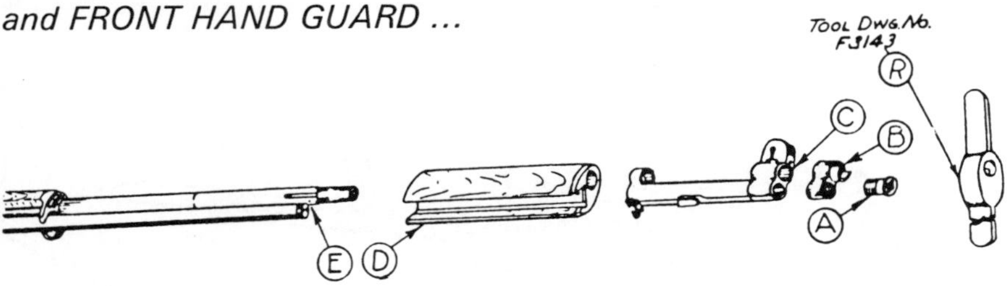

7. Unscrew the gas cylinder lock screw (A) and gas cylinder lock (B). Remove the gas cylinder assembly (C) and front hand guard (D) by sliding them off the end of the rifle barrel (E). Should the cylinder lock (B) be tight, draw off with tool (R).

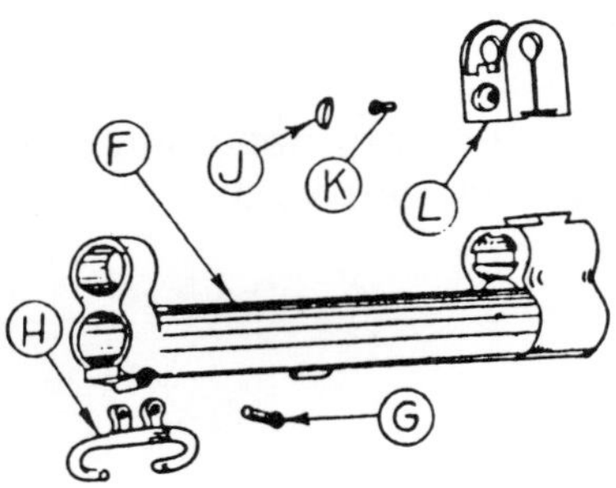

8. To dismantle the gas cylinder assembly (F), remove the swivel screw (G) and stock swivel (H). Pry off the front sight screw seal (J), unscrew the front sight screw (K) and then remove the front sight (L).

REMOVAL OF OPERATING ROD SPRING and FOLLOWER ROD ...

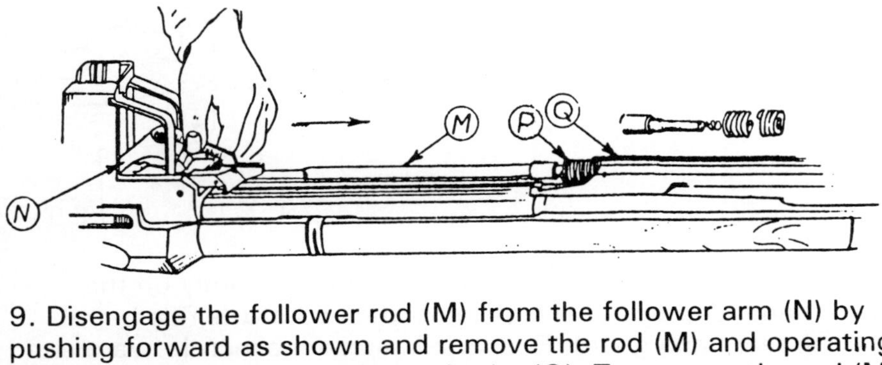

9. Disengage the follower rod (M) from the follower arm (N) by pushing forward as shown and remove the rod (M) and operating spring (P) from the operating rod tube (Q). To remove the rod (M) from the spring (P), twist and pull apart.

REMOVAL OF OPERATING ROD HANDLE from RECEIVER GROUP ...

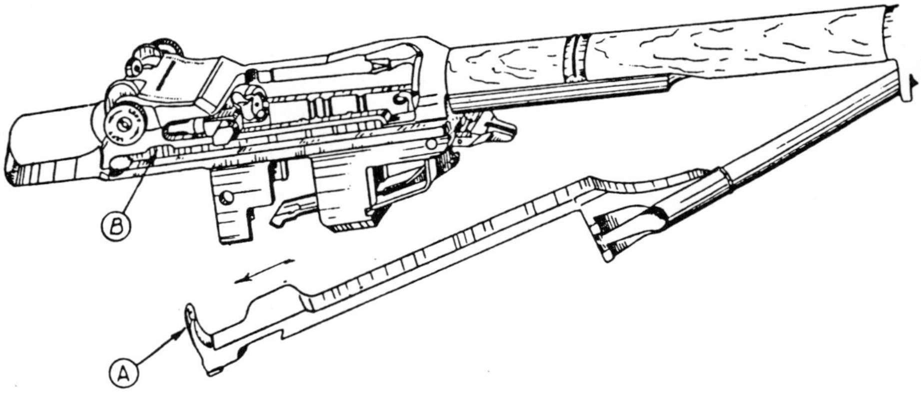

10. Hold the operating rod handle (A) in the right hand and slide it back to position (B) and pull it up and then outward.

REMOVAL OF REAR HAND GUARD ...

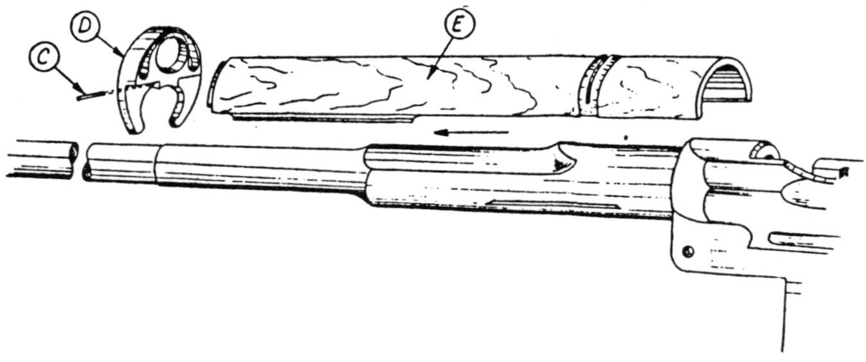

11. Punch out the lower band pin (C) and tap evenly on the lower band (D), loosen and slide off the end of the rifle barrel. Pull the rear hand guard (E) approximately one inch forward and twist off.

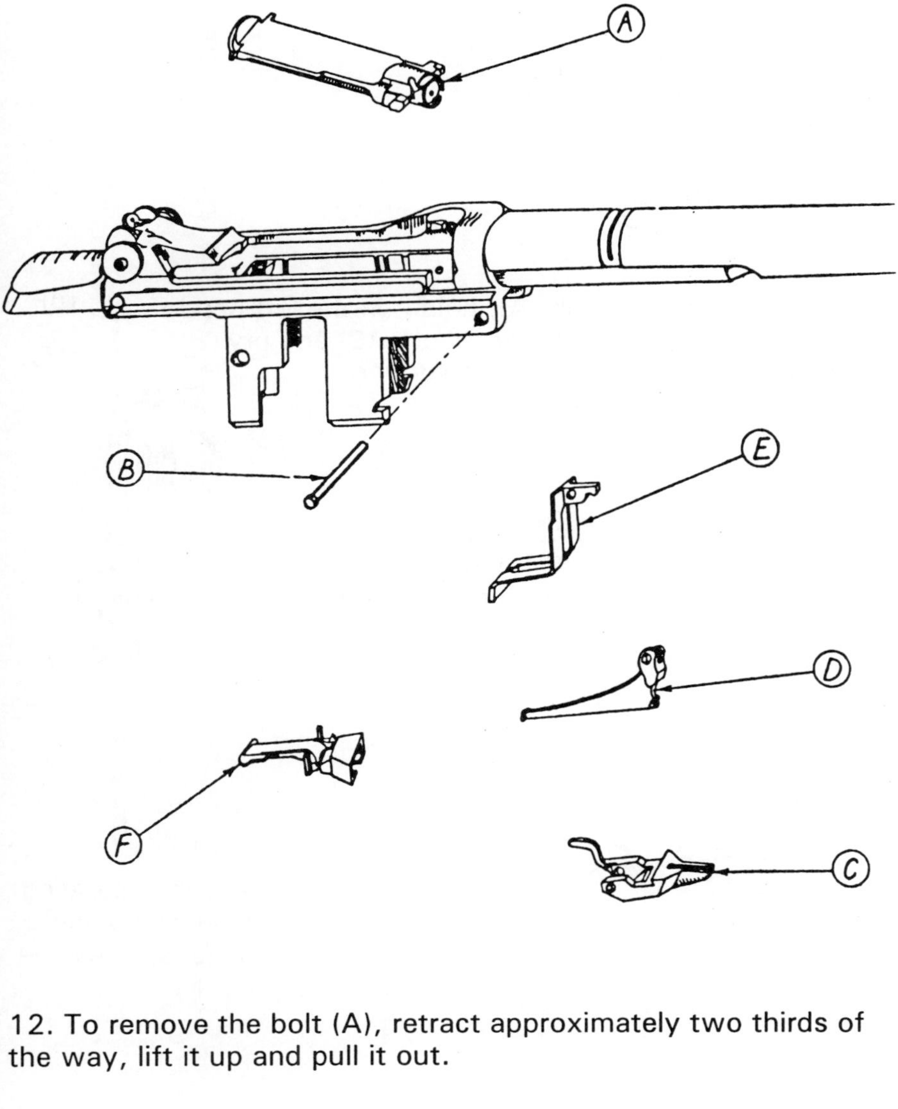

12. To remove the bolt (A), retract approximately two thirds of the way, lift it up and pull it out.

13. By punching out the follower arm pin (B), the operating rod catch assembly (C), follower arm (D), bullet guide (E) and follower slide assmebly (F) can now be removed.

DISMANTLING of BOLT, ACCELERATOR and FOLLOWER ASSEMBLY ...

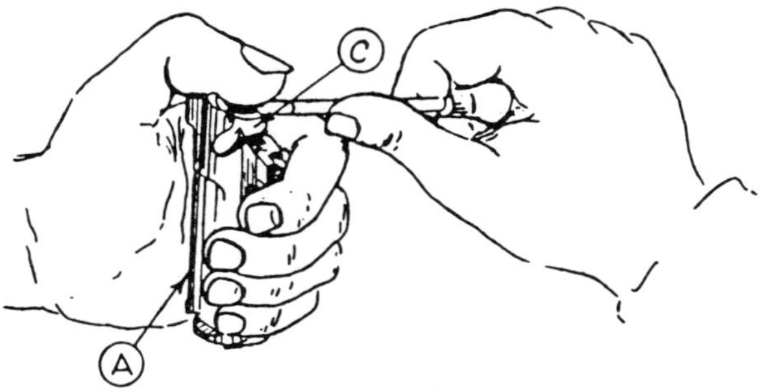

14. To dismantle the bolt (A), hold it in the left hand with thumb over the cartridge ejector (B) and pry out on the extractor with a screwdriver.

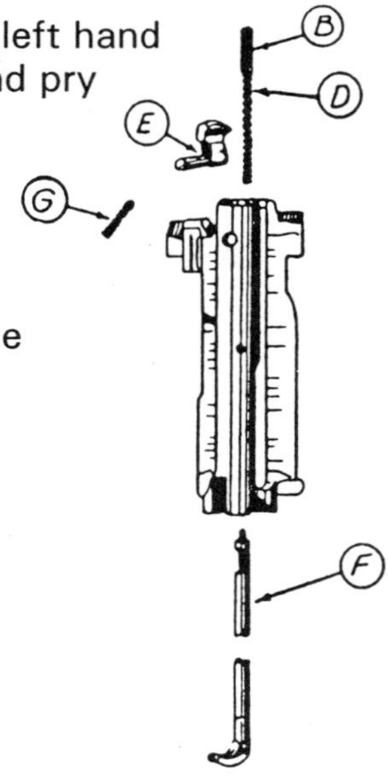

15. The mechanism is now unlocked and the cartridge ejector spring (D), extractor (E), firing pin (F) and extractor plunger spring (G) can be removed as shown at right.

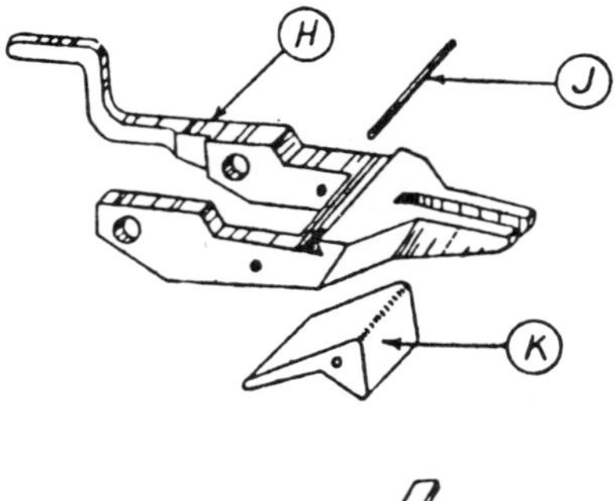

16. To dismantle the operating rod catch (H), punch out the accelerator pin (J) and remove the accelerator (K).

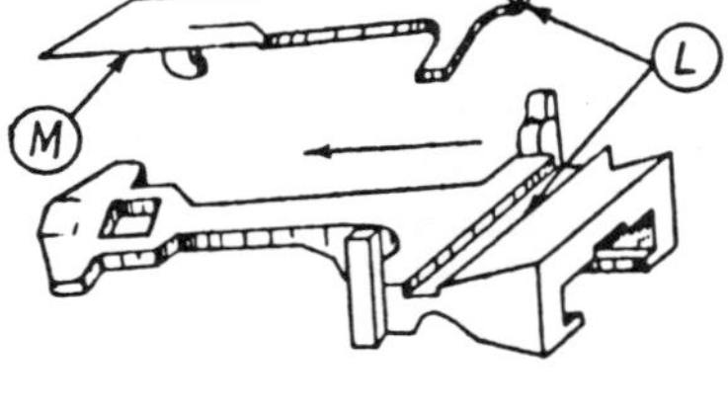

17. Unlock the follower assembly by inserting a screwdriver under the end (L), lift and pry it forward on the follower slide (M) and remove.

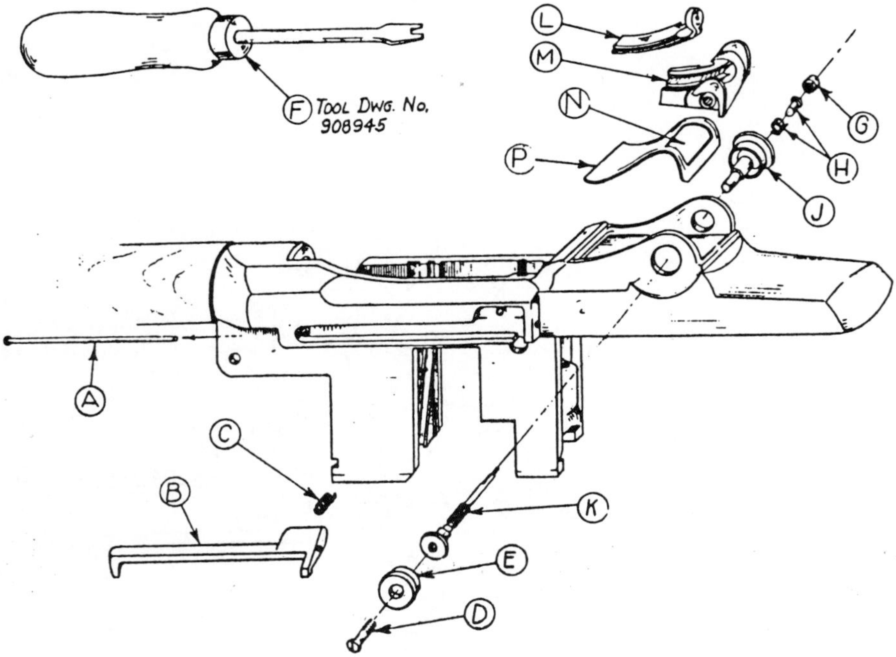

18. To remove the clip latch, punch out the latch pin (A) and remove the clip latch (B) and latch spring (C).

19. Unscrew sight screw (D) and remove elevating knob (E). With a split screw driver (F) take out the rear sight nut (G), lock and spring (H). Unscrew the rear sight windage knob (J) and push out the sight and elevating pinion (K).

20. Remove aperture (L) from rear sight base (M). Insert screw driver in slot (N) and pry up. Pull the base (M) from the sight cover (P).

Note: Dismantling the barrel from the receiver requires placing the barrel knox form in a fixture and removal of the receiver, in a counter-clockwise direction, with a wrench placed on the receiver as close to the barrel as possible.

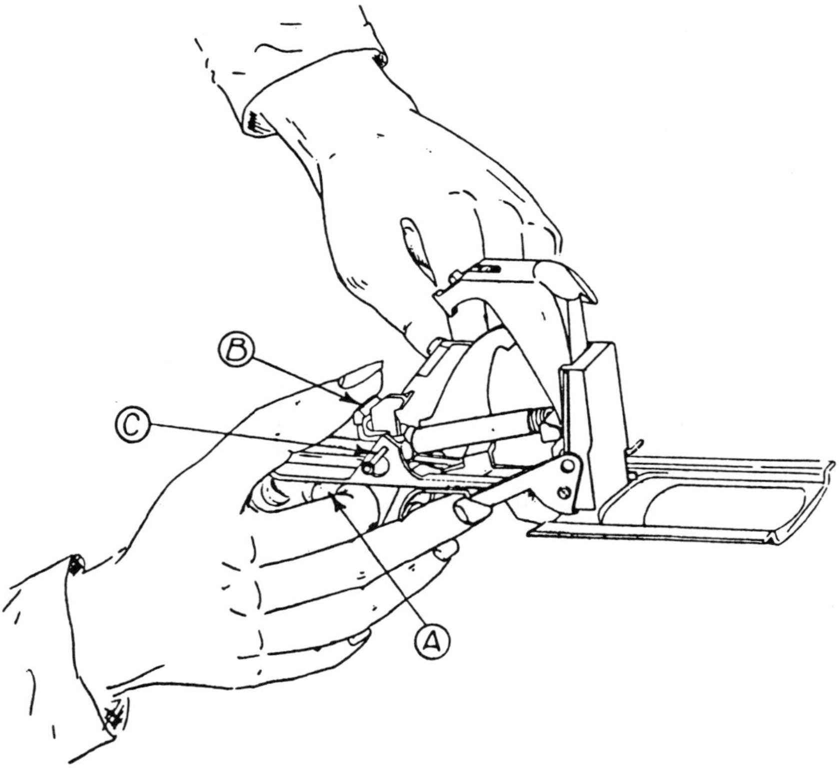

21. Holding the trigger housing and assembled parts in the right hand as shown, with right fore-finger depressing the trigger (A) and right thumb bearing down on the sear (B), drift out the trigger pin (C). Withdraw the punch and relieve tension of the assembled parts slowly.

22. After the pin (C) has been drifted out, lift out of the trigger (A). To remove sar (D) punch out pin (E).

Note: Sear (D) should not be removed from trigger (D) unless damaged.

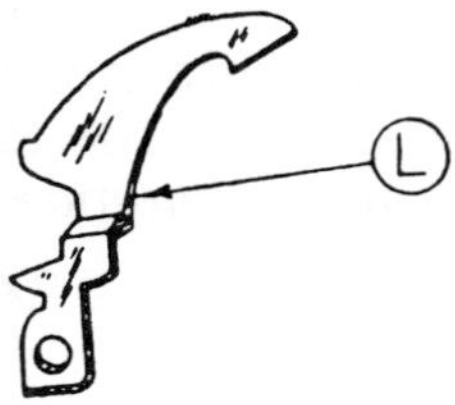

23. Take out hammer spring housing (F). Pull out the spring (H) and plunger (J) from the housing (F).

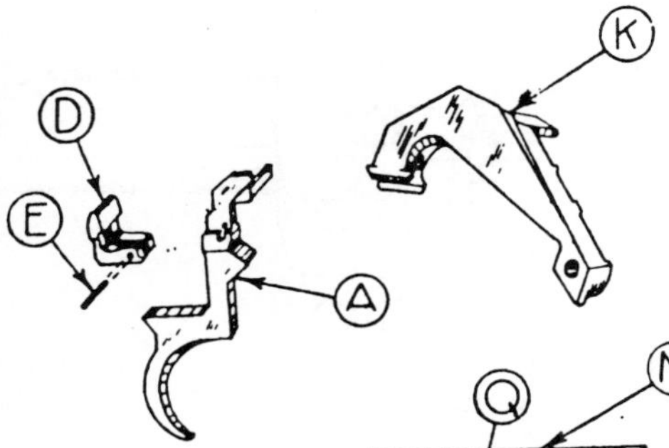

24. Punch out the hammer pin (G) and remove the hammer (K). Pull out on safety (L), and lift up.

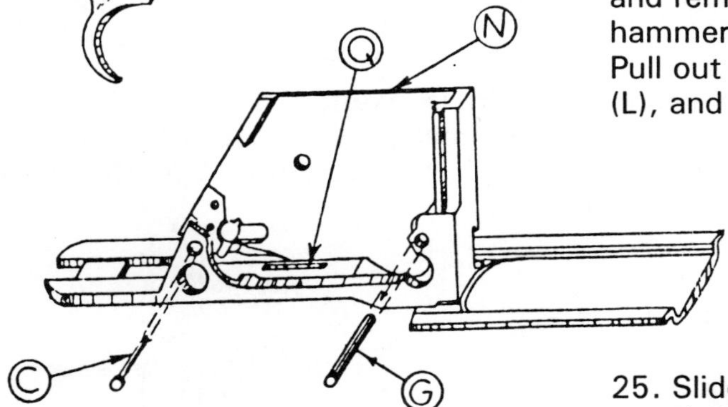

25. Slide trigger guard (M) to rear and downward, canting it to the right so that it falls clear of the housing (N).

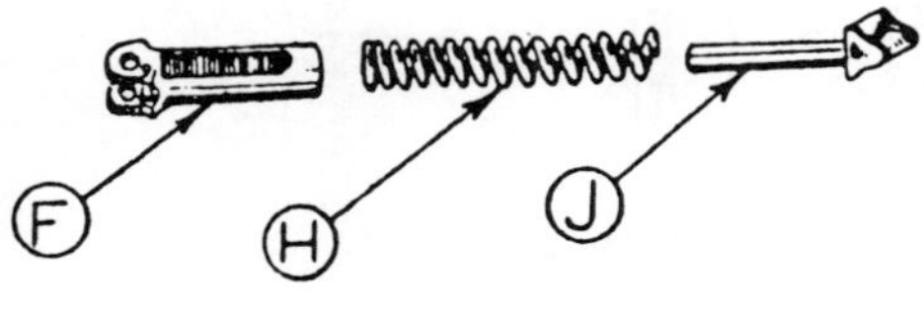

26. To remove the clip ejector (P), place a screwdriver between the ejector and trigger housing (N) at position (Q) and then twist the screwdriver.

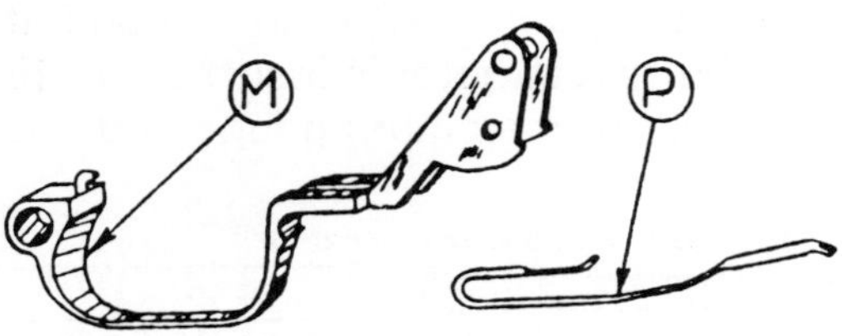

All parts are to be cleaned, dried, burrs removed, and checked for any cracked or broken parts. *Note: The tool drawing nos. preceded by 'F' are Frankfort Arsenal numbers.*

1. Insert bolt in receiver and slip a 1.946-in. gauge (A) in the breech and close bolt. If bolt lug (B) will slide to edge of the shoulder (C) as shown at right; the headspace is sufficient for maximum test.

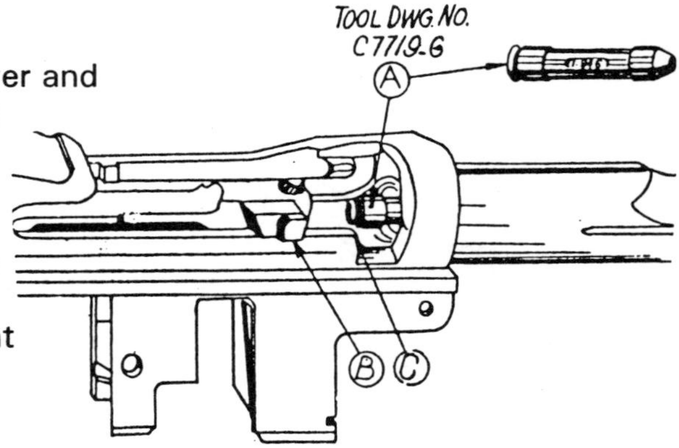

2. The minimum gauge 1.940-in. is inserted. If the bolt lug will go down all the way and move freely, headspace is sufficient and the bore of the barrel is ready for checking. *Note:* Check the bore before reaming headspace.

3. To check the bore, place the tool (D) in the breech as shown at right and inspect for rust, metal foulings, usage, pits and crimps. To check for usage, insert a .30 gauge through the barrel; if it slides smoothly, the barrel has the proper bore.

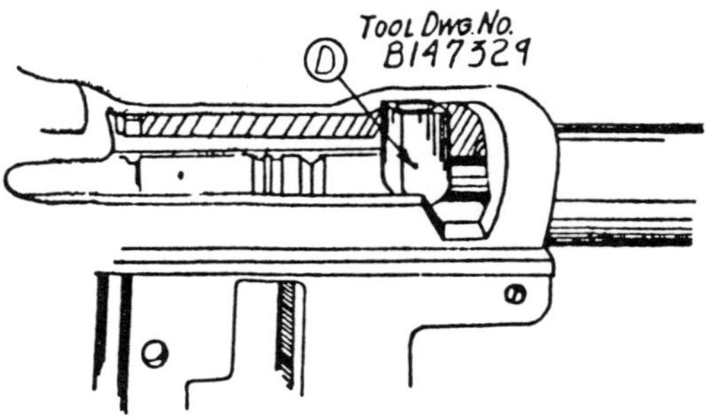

If a .30 gauge fits tightly, minimum gauge .2998-in. is used; if it will not go through smoothly, barrel diameter is insufficient. If a .30 gauge fits loosely, use a .302-in. maximum gauge and if it fits too loosely, barrel is rejected.

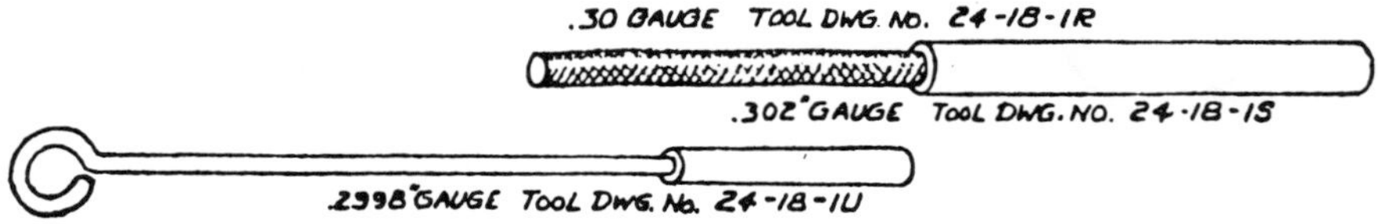

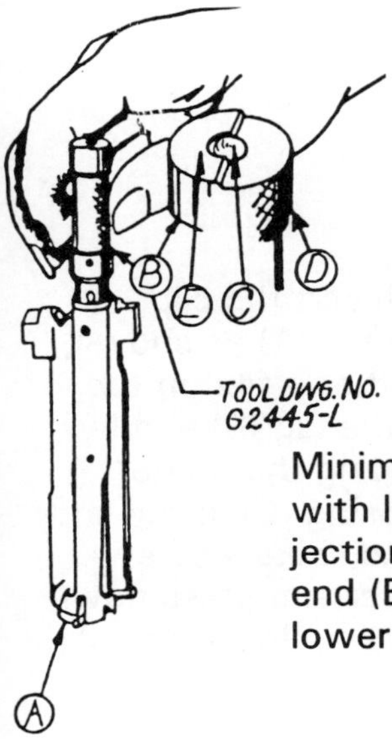

4. Insert the firing pin (A) in the bolt. To check firing pin, hold bolt with front end up in the left hand. Ensure the end of the firing pin is resting on a flat surface. Place the gauge (B) over point of firing pin and press downward, bringing end of gauge against face of the bolt. The flush pin (C) in the gauge is forced into position, indicating the projection of the firing pin on the bolt face.

Minimum projection is indicated when pin is flush with lower step (D) on gauge (B). Maximum projection is indicated when the pin is with the upper end (E) of the gauge. Reject if pin is below the lower step or projects above the end of the gauge.

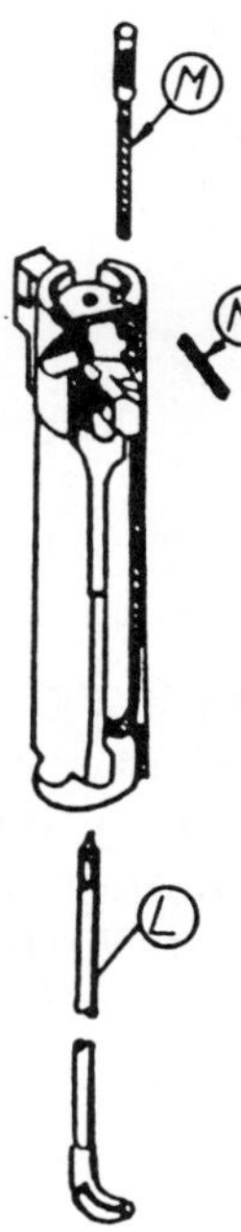

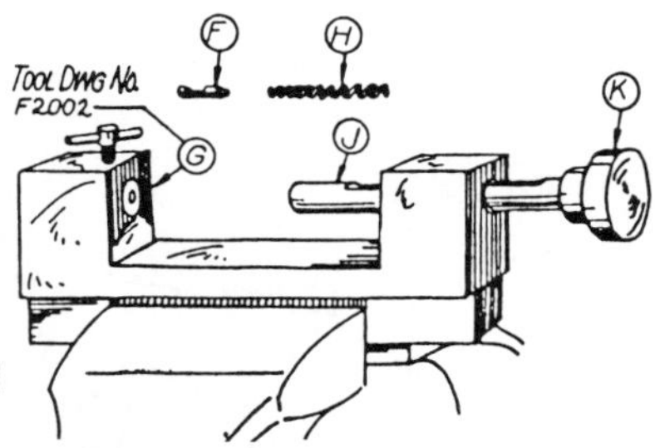

5. Insert the ejector (F) in the hole in the fixture at (G). Insert spring (H) in shaft (J). Press on knob (K), inserting ejector in the spring. Insert the firing pin (L) first, then the cartridge ejector (M), and the extractor spring (N).

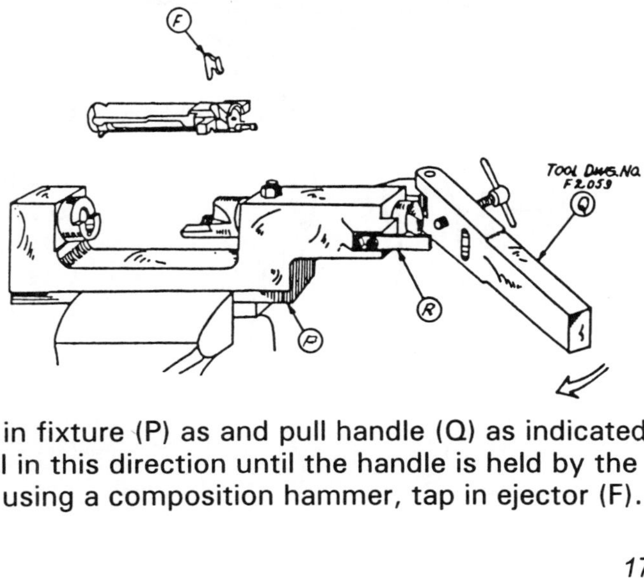

6. Insert the bolt in fixture (P) as and pull handle (Q) as indicated by the arrow. Pull in this direction until the handle is held by the spring (R). Then, using a composition hammer, tap in ejector (F).

TRIGGER GROUP ASSEMBLY ...

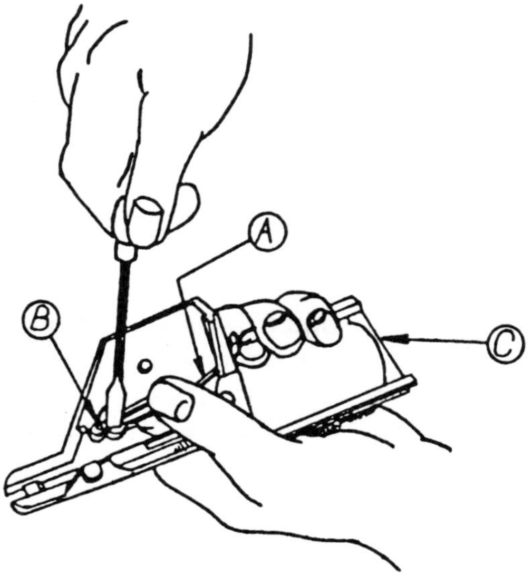

7. Insert the clip ejector (A) as shown, so that it fits on top of the lug (B) and by holding the trigger housing (C) in the left hand, take a screw-driver and press down on the clip ejector (A).

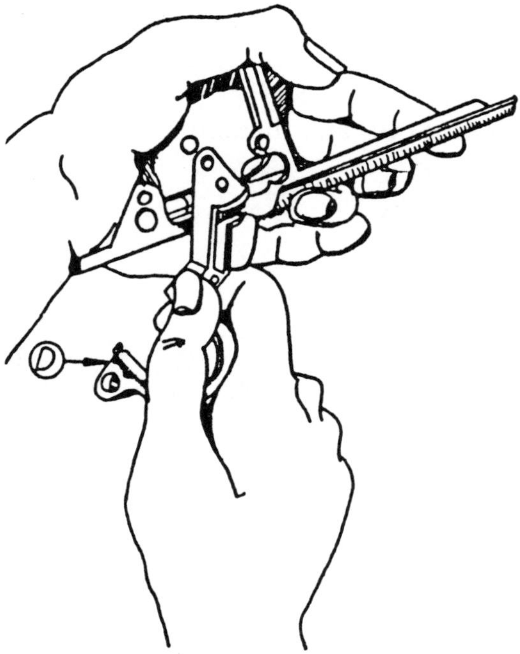

8. Place the trigger guard (D) on the housing by tilting the guard at right angles to the housing. Push it forward into position. Check to see that the holes are in alignment.

9. Insert the safety (A) by downward pressure, with the lug (B) facing the wall of the housing, and it will slip into the hole (C) on the side of the housing. *Note:* Be sure the safety (A) is in straight up and down before continuing.

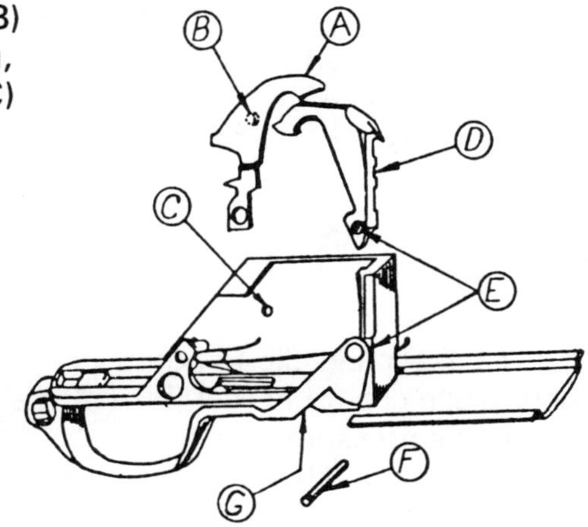

Insert the hammer (D) with shoulders facing the wall of the housing and line up the holes (E) for hammer pin (F). Insert the pin (F) with the head of the pin on the right side of the housing and tap it into position to lock the trigger guard (G) and hammer (D) in housing.

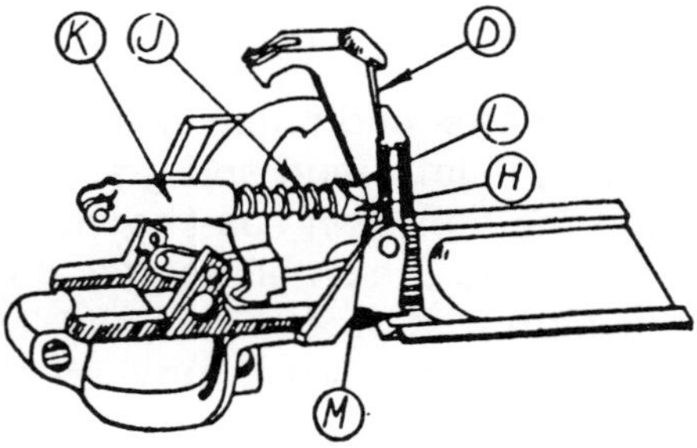

10. Push the hammer (D) forward and the guard automatically comes up. Take the hammer spring plunger (H), slip it into the hammer spring (J) and fit the two into the hammer spring housing (K); hold them together and slip the groove (L) into the notch (M). *Note:* Be sure that the opening on the hammer spring housing faces the wall of the trigger housing.

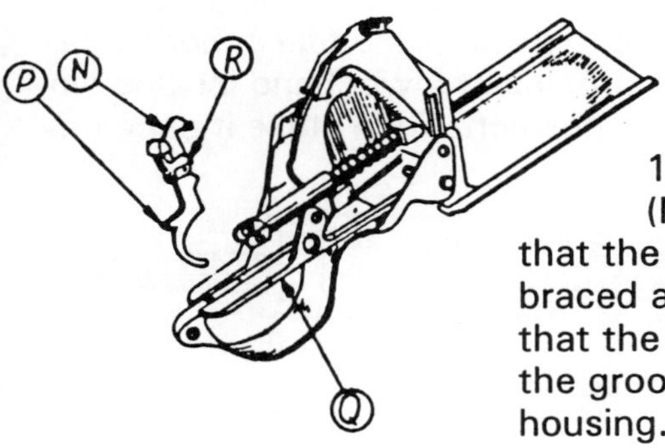

11. Insert the trigger group (N) into position, making sure that the shoulder (P) on the trigger is braced against the housing (Q) and that the lugs (R) on the sear enter the grooves in the hammer spring housing.

12. Place index finger of left hand on trigger (A) and thumb on lock of sear (B). By pulling trigger, group (C) will slide into position as shown. Insert trigger pin (D) and tap into position. In assembly, heel of trigger should rest on the housing.

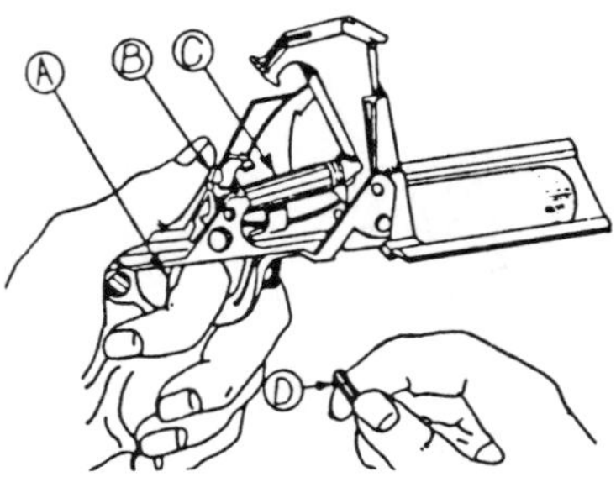

13. To assemble clip to handgrip, place clip (E) in tool (F) and apply pressure at (G). Place handgrip (H) in the opened clip and insert tool (J) inside handgrip. Release pressure at (G).

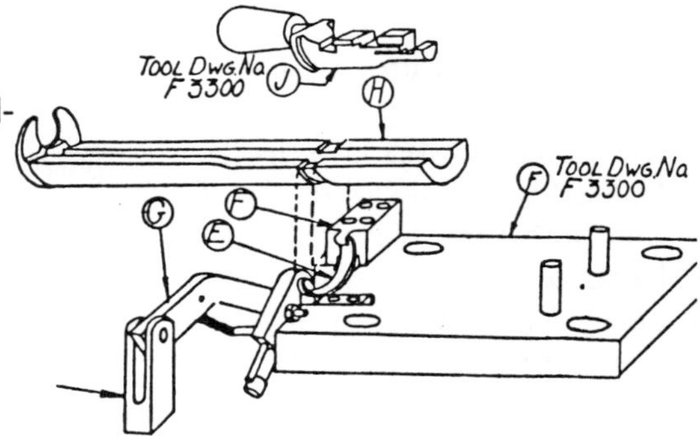

14. Place barrel and receiver in vertical position. Hold barrel in left hand and grasping rear hand guard in the right hand as shown, push forward and slide the small flanges on the band (K) into the grooves (L) and (M). Then, using a downward movement, slide base of handguard until it rests against shoulder (N) of the receiver.

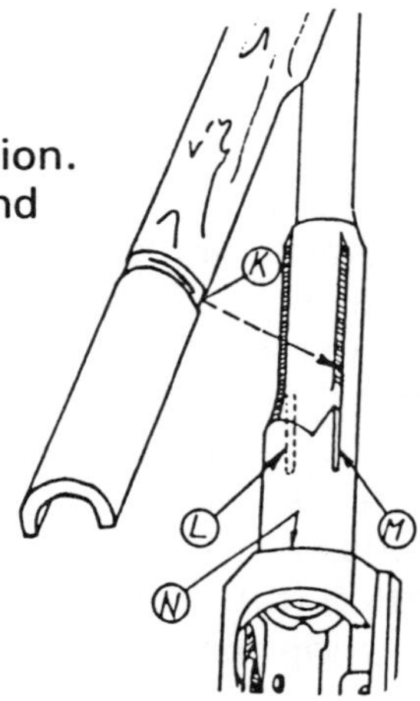

15. Drop lower band ferrule over end of the barrel, tap into place with tool (A^1) as below. Remove tool and place rifle in horizontal position (with underside facing up). Insert lower band locking pin (B^1) from either side and tap into position. Then stake it once on each side.

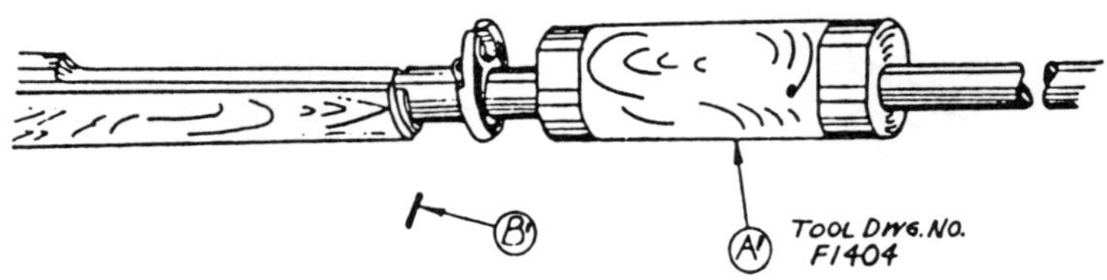

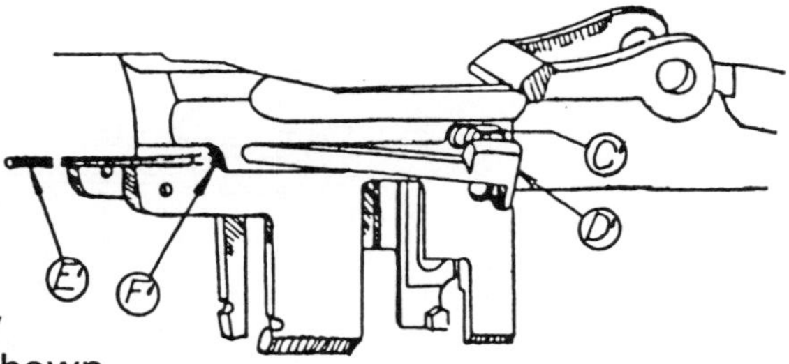

16. Place clip latch spring (C[1]) into position as shown at right. Place rifle on its right side. Lay clip latch in receiver as shown and while pushing on (D[1]) with the right hand, push clip latch pin (E[1]) with left hand into hole (F[1]), locking clip latch into position.

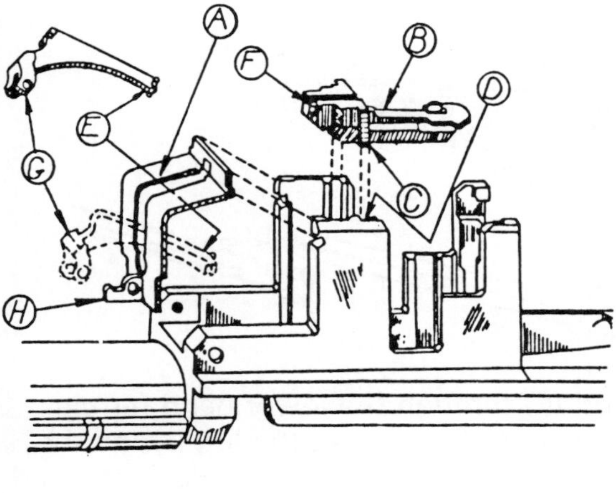

17. Place rifle upside down and insert bullet guide (A) as shown. Place follower (B) with shoulders (C) in the grooves (D) and insert follower arm by tilting it until lugs (E) pass through the gap in the bullet guide, slide lugs (E) into grooves (F) in the follower.

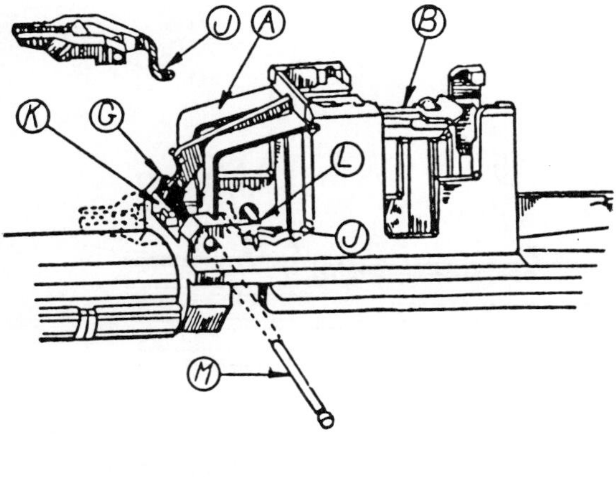

Lower end (G) over lug (H). Insert operating rod latch (J) as shown at left, through the opening (K) and place under latch clip (L). Insert follower arm pin (M) to lock receiver assembly.

ASSEMBLY (Cont'd.)...

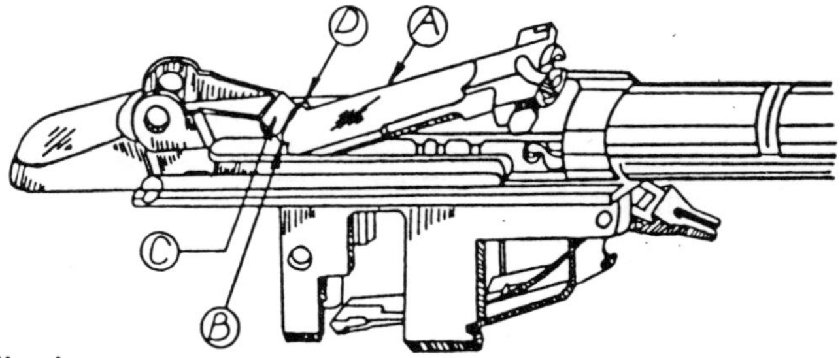

18. Place rifle right side up. Tilt the rear end of bolt (A) down, slide flange (B) under projector (C), at the same time pushing lug (D) down through the notch. Push the bolt to the rear of the receiver.

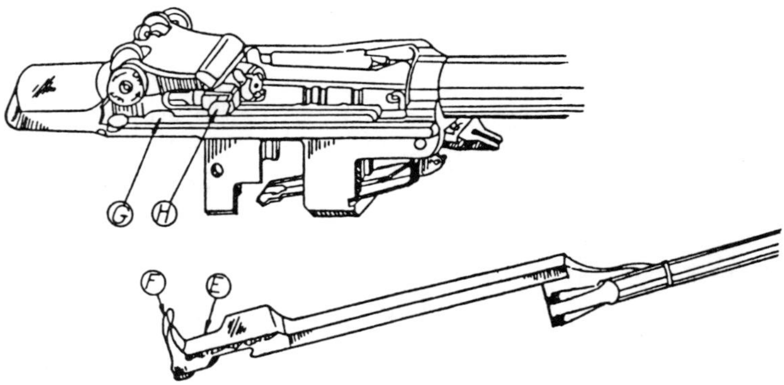

19. Place the operating rod (E) through the lower band ferrule. Bring the handle (F) into position (G), so that the lug (H) on the bolt will fit unto the shoulder on the operating rod. Push forward on the handle, locking the two together.

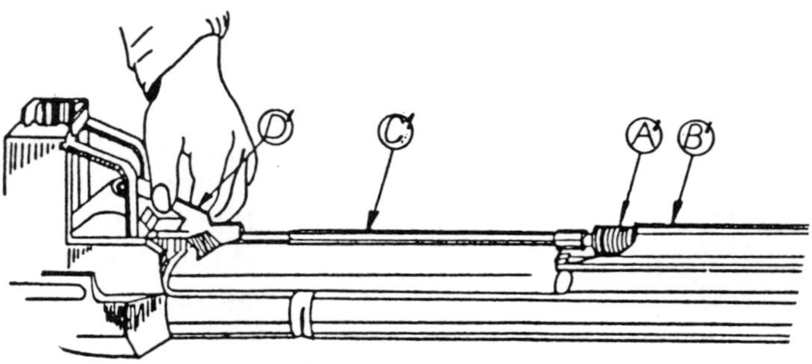

20. Place the spring (A^1) in the operating rod (B^1) and place the follower rod (C^1) onto the follower arm (D^1) as shown above.

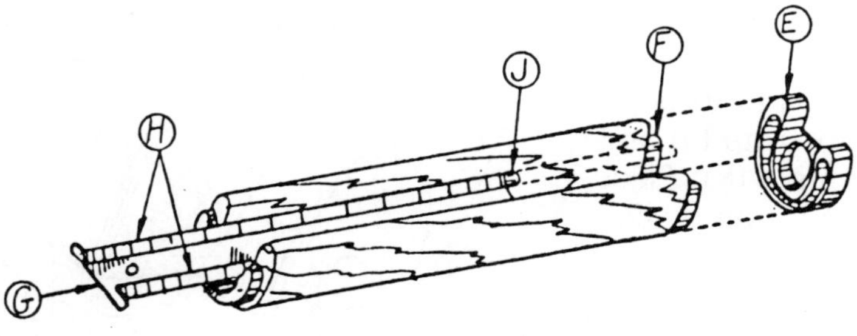

21. Place front band guard ferrule (E) on the front hand guard (F) and tap it on with a hammer, making sure it is tight. Then insert front hand guard spacer (G) with flanges (H) extending upward toward the open slot in the forward hand guard. Tap spacer (G) into the seat so that front ears (J) can be locked over the ferrule.

Note: Press on bottom of spacer while locking ears on the ferrule. The hand guard is then placed on the barrel, ferrule end toward the muzzle, and pressed into the rear hand guard ferrule.

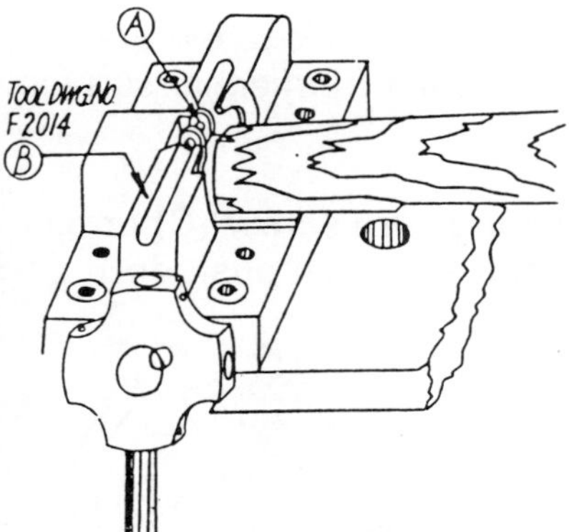

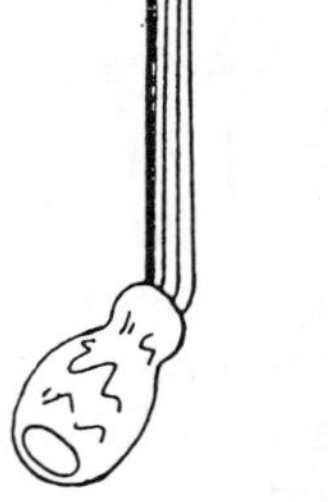

22. Place the stock [C46013] ferrule (A) in the left end of the fixture (B) as shown above with the hole (C) in the butt of the stock over the lug (D). Turn the handle on the right end of the fixture (B), forcing the tip of the stock into the ferrule (A). The ears of the ferrule (A) are then brought together by rotating the handle at the left end of the fixture (B). Remove the stock from the fixture.

23. Place the stock ferrule swivel on the ears of the ferrule and insert the screw from the right side of the stock. Tighten so that the swivel does not move too freely.

24. Place spring (E) on plunger (F), insert both in gate (G). Holding index finger over plunger (F), place parts through (H) in butt plate (J) and insert cap pin (K). Place butt plate (J) on stock (L) and insert small screw (M) at heel of stock. Insert butt swivel (N) in slot (P), slide in screw (Q) and screw tight.

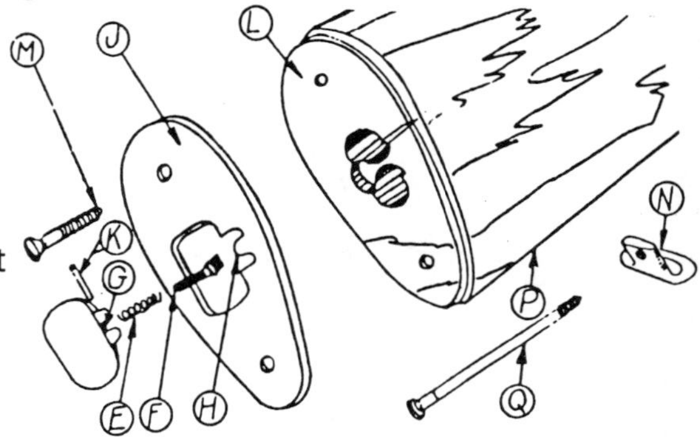

ASSEMBLE GAS CYLINDER ...

25. Inspect inside of gas cylinder (A) for carbon and pitting. If carbon is present, take wire brush with extension and clean out. Run a dry patch through the chamber. Be sure head of piston and base of gas cylinder lock screw are clean of carbon and no metal has been chipped from either surface.

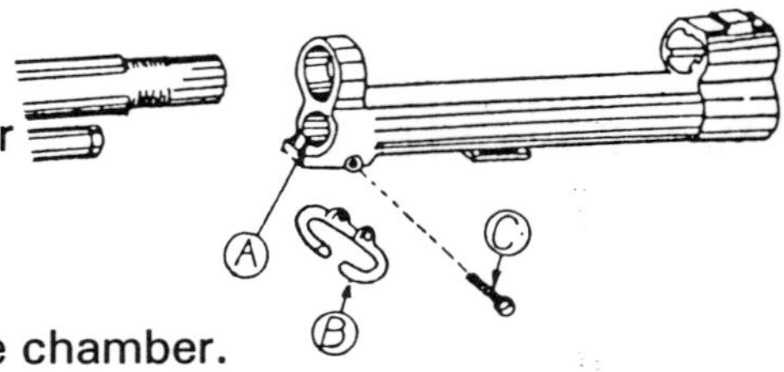

26. Assemble stacking swivel (B), making sure screw (C) enters from the right side when rifle is held in the normal position.

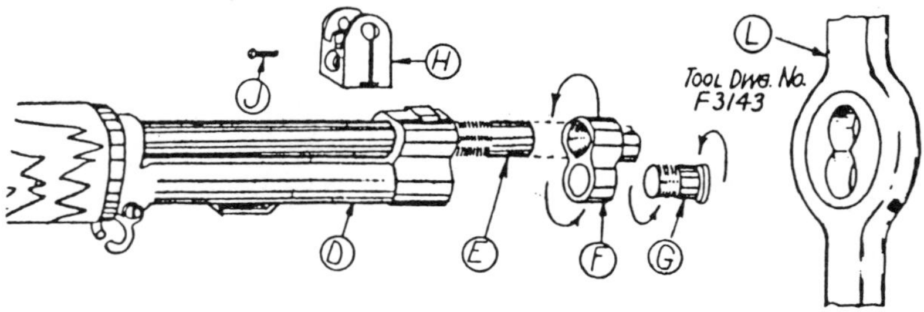

27. Slide gas cylinder (D) on barrel (E) checking to see cylinder is turned so front sight space is in correct position. Place gas cylinder lock (F) on barrel and screw on using special tool (L). Screw (F) against shoulder of (D), back off until aligned for insertion of (G). Screw in gas cylinder lock screw (G) and tighten.

28. Assemble front sight (H) by sliding into approximate center, noting that space for the seal cover is facing the rear, and insert screw (J). Tighten screw up, fairly tight.

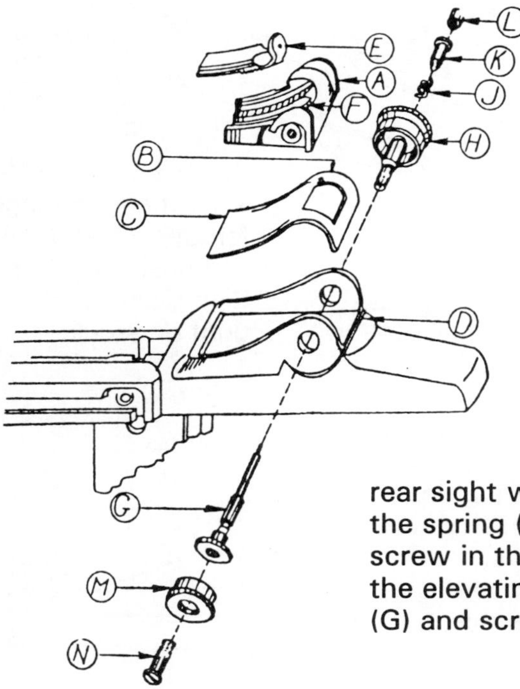

29. Insert rear sight base (A) into the cover spring (B) and, with the end (C) first in the rifle, applying pressure on the rear of the sight base (A) until it snaps into the groove (D). Push the aperture (E) in the space at (F).

30. Insert the sight elevating pinion (G) and screw on the rear sight windage knob (H). Place the spring (J) on the lock (K) and screw in the rear sight nut (L). Place the elevating knob (M) over pinion (G) and screw in sight screw (N).

31. After the rifle is completely assembled, place it in a fixture (P) [F1930] as shown with the two screws (Q) [A13677] and (R) [A13678] directly under the punches (S) and (T) and tap the ends of punches hard enough to stake the screws.

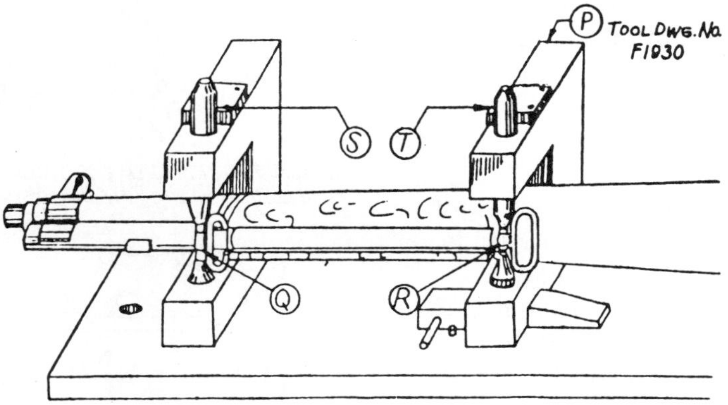

RE-ASSEMBLY...
Receiver & Barrel,
Stock & Trigger
Housing groups.

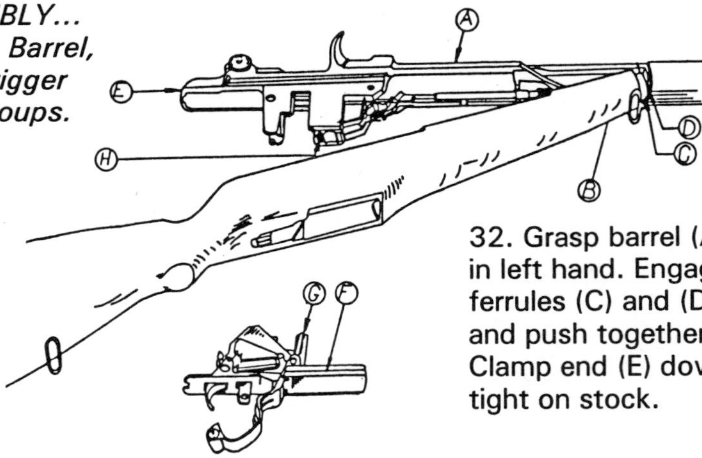

32. Grasp barrel (A) in left hand. Engage ferrules (C) and (D) and push together. Clamp end (E) down tight on stock.

33. Insert trigger housing (F) through stock recess to engage receiver group, noting that lugs (G) slide into grooves (H). After it is in position, push down on trigger guard until it locks.
Note: Cock trigger before inserting trigger housing group into stock, by pulling down on trigger guard.

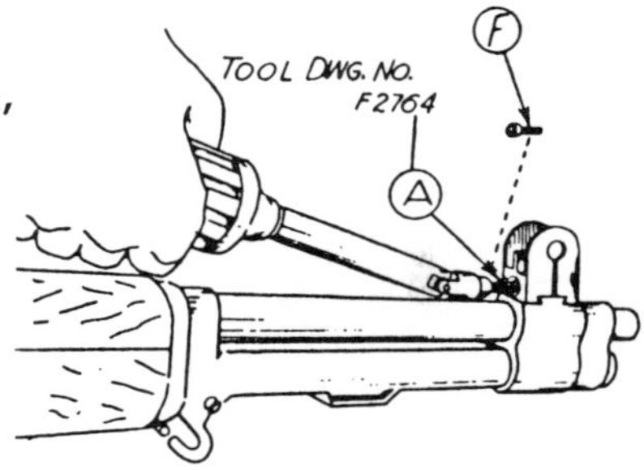

FIG. 1

34. Set front sight flush with left side of gas cylinder (A). Rifle is then held in fixed rest, composed of cradle, drawing No. SA.13929. Two or three shots are fired on target and adjustments are made to bring the sight into agreement.
Note: Only ten per cent of the rifles are so targeted.

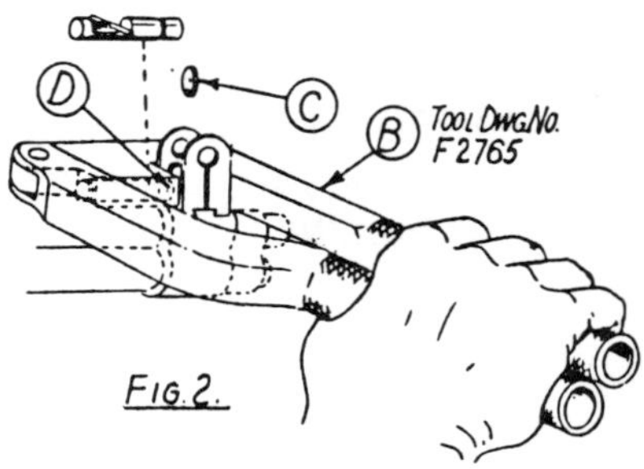

FIG. 2.

NOTE: FIXTURE AS IN FIG.3, OR ONE SIMILAR MAY BE USED FOR HOLDING RIFLE IN A FIXED REST.

35. After the rifle has front sight set as noted above, screw (F) is tightened as shown at Fig. 1. Using tool (B) as shown in Fig. 2, place seal over space (D) and press into place. *Note:* Fixture as in Fig. 3, or one similar, may be used for holding rifle in a fixed rest.

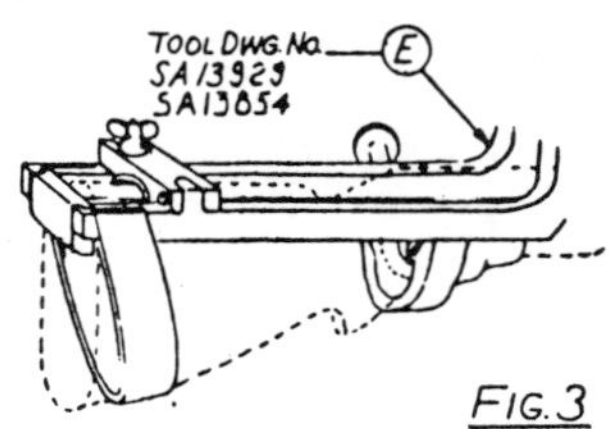

FIG. 3

SERVICE & MAINTENANCE...

Cleaning is the most important aspect of maintaining the M1 rifle. Proper maintenance extends life and reduces malfunctions.

Stock & other wooden parts...
Wipe exterior with dry cloth to remove damp, dirt or perspiration. Wipe stock and handguards with Oil, linseed, raw. Keep linseed oil away from operating parts, it hardens and prevents functioning.

Metal surfaces...
To clean screw heads and crevices, use a small cleaning brush or stick. To clean surfaces, wipe with dry cloth to remove wet, dirt or perspiration, then wipe with cloth moistened with Oil, lubricating, preservative, light. This film should be maintained at all times.

Cleaning preparatory to firing...
1. Dismount main groups.
2. Clean and oil the bore very lightly, do not oil the chamber.
3. Remove any carbon on the gas cylinder plug and piston head.
4. Thoroughly clean and lightly oil all metal parts.
5. Well lubricate the bolt lugs, bolt guides, cocking cam on bolt, compensating spring, contact surfaces of barrel and operating rod, operating rod cam, operating rod guide groove in receiver, and operating rod spring.
6. Do not apply lubricating grease to the follower slide or under surface of the bolt as the introduction of grease into the chamber may lead to the generation of excessive pressure.

Cleaning after firing...
Rifles should be cleaned not later than the evening of the day on which they are fired, but preferably immediately after firing. Complete cleaning should be done with the groups dismounted.
1. Bore & chamber. The bore should be thoroughly cleaned with bore-cleaning fluid. Insert a clean patch in the slot in the cleaning rod and saturate it with cleaner. Insert the cleaning rod from the muzzle end and push the patch back and forth through the bore several times. Be sure the patch goes all the way though the bore before the direction is reversed.
2. Gas Cylinder & Gas Cylinder Plug. Excessive deposits of carbon manifest themselves by sluggishness in action and failure to feed. Remove carbon with screwdriver blade of combination tool. Do not remove gas cylinder for cleaning. It is cleaned with the cleaning rod and patch, similar to how the bore is cleaned.

OPERATION & FUNCTION...

LOADING the CARTRIDGE CLIP...
Eight rounds are inserted in the clip so the cartridge extractor groove engages the inner rib of the clip. Unless the base of each round is against the rear wall of the clip, cartridges may protrude so far forward that insertion of the clip in the rifle receiver is prevented. The top round should be on the right, facing forward.

LOADING the RIFLE...
Hold the rifle at point of balance in the left hand. With forefinger of right hand, pull the operating rod handle smartly to the rear until the rod is caught by its catch. With the right hand, place a fully loaded clip on top of the follower.

Then place the right thumb on the middle of the top cartridge, press the cartridge clip down into the receiver until it engages the clip latch. Swing the thumb to the right so as to clear the bolt in its forward movement. Closing the bolt may be assisted by striking the operating rod handle forward with the heel of the right hand.

With a little practice, loading a clip containing less than eight rounds can be done easily. Using the right forefinger to hold the rounds down against bottom lips of the clip, a partially loaded clip is placed on top of follower. Rounds are held in place and the clip allowed to drop down until the top cartridges are against the upper lips of the clip.

With right thumb on top of the rounds and right side of the right hand pressing the operating rod handle slightly to the rear, press the clip down into the receiver until it engages the clip latch. Swing thumb to the right to clear the bolt in its forward movement. Release operating rod handle.

Moving the operating rod to the rear cocks the hammer. The barrel chamber is loaded when the bolt moves forward, stripping the top round from the clip. Moving the safety to the rear in the trigger bow locks the hammer and trigger.

FIRING...

With safety off (pushed forward), bolt locked home and round in the chamber, pressing the trigger releases the cocked hammer. When the hammer flies forward, it strikes the rear of the firing pin and detonates the cartridge primer. As the bullet travels down the bore and passes the gas port, gasses enter the gas cylinder and drive the operating rod to the rear, compressing the rod spring. Its cam surfaces contact the bolt lug, to rotate and move it to the rear, extracting and ejecting the fired case.

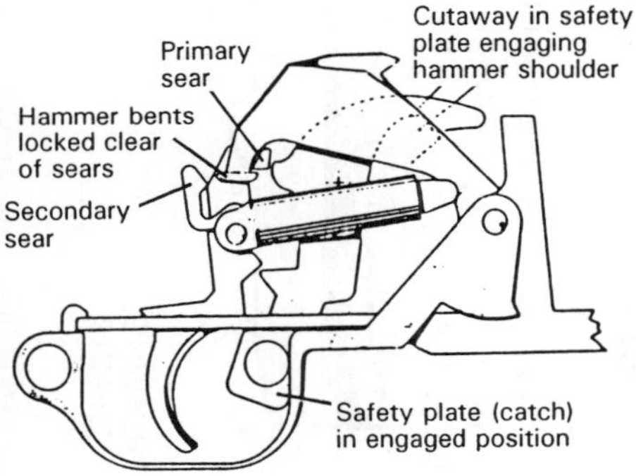

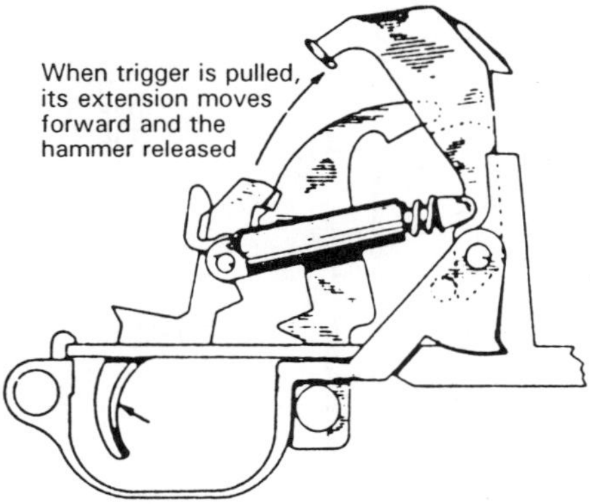

During the rearward travel of the bolt, the hammer is forced back to the cocked position, with the hammer coil spring again compressed. Upon return of the bolt and operating rod forward, caused by the compressed operating rod spring, the top round is stripped from the clip and loaded into the chamber, in readiness to repeat the cycle.

After the clip is emptied and thrown clear by the clip ejector; the operating rod is held to the rear to permit loading of another clip. Repeat the procedure on the previous page to continue firing.

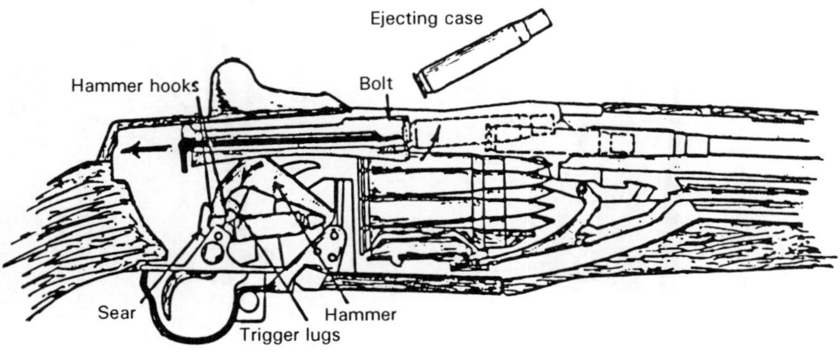

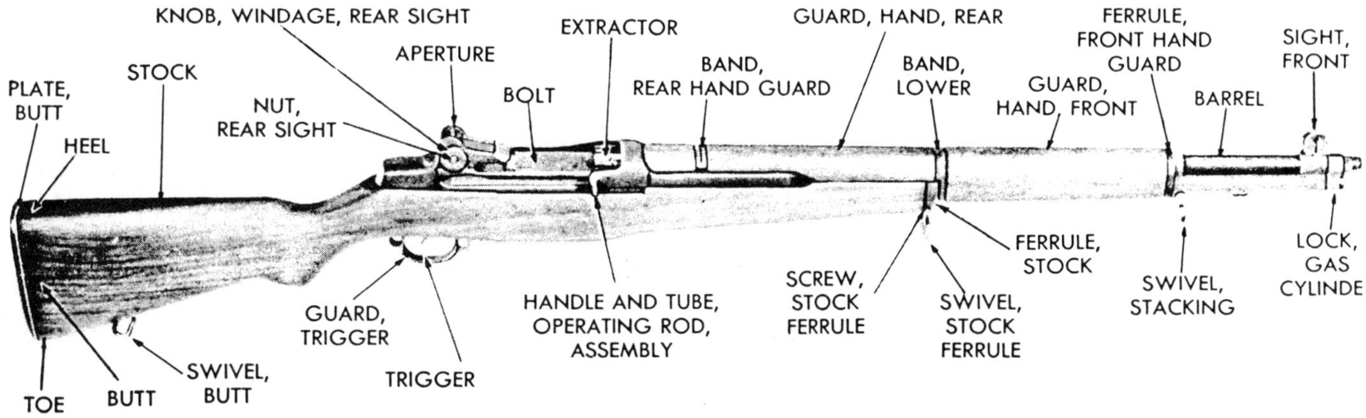

U.S. .30 Cal. M1 Garand rifle external component parts

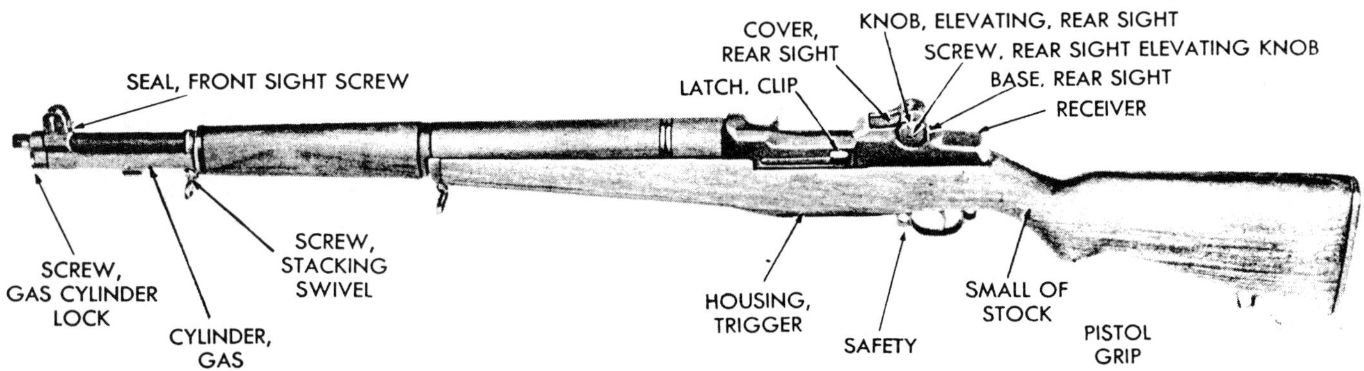

Detail Stripping

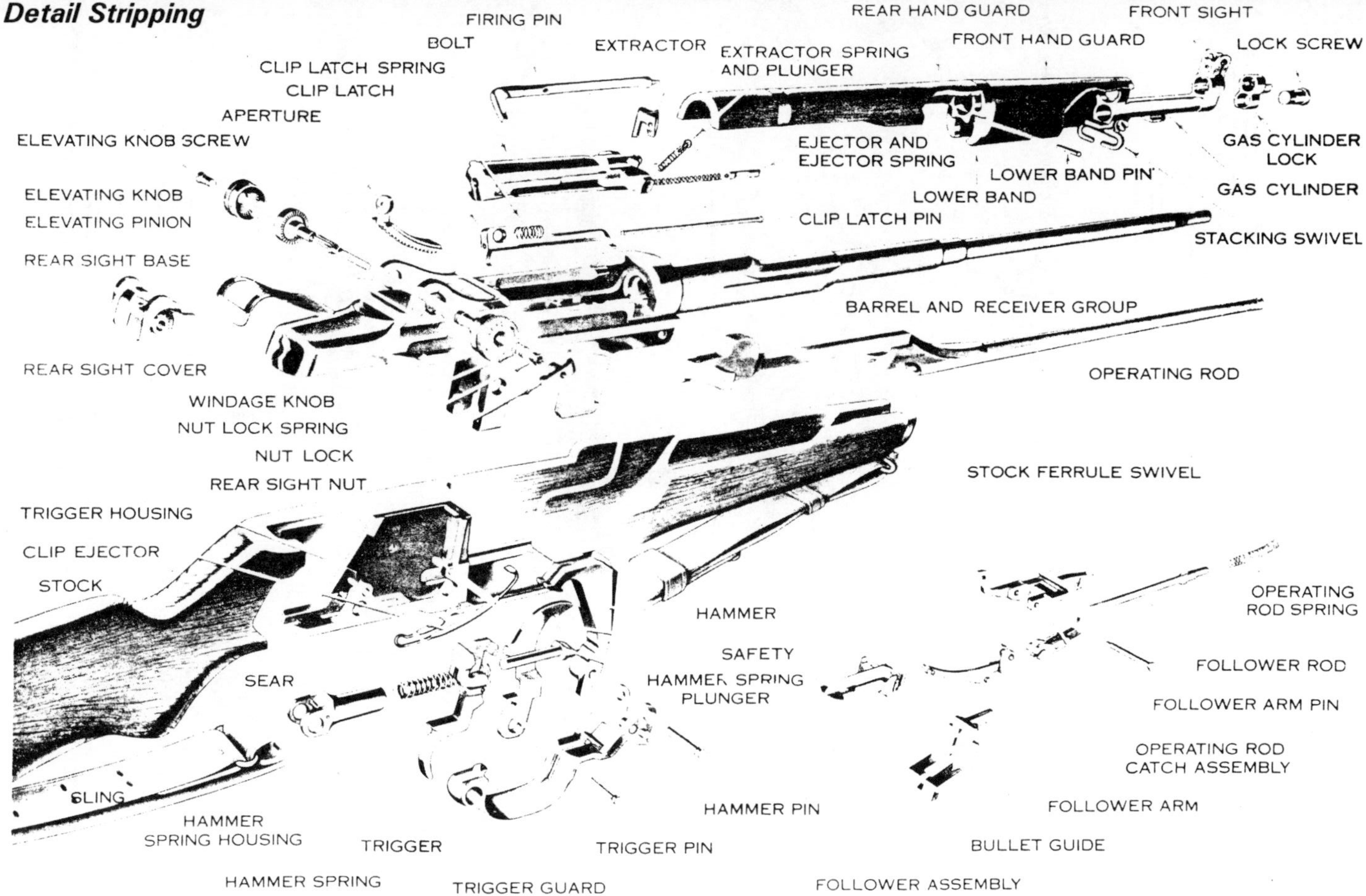

ACCESSORIES ...

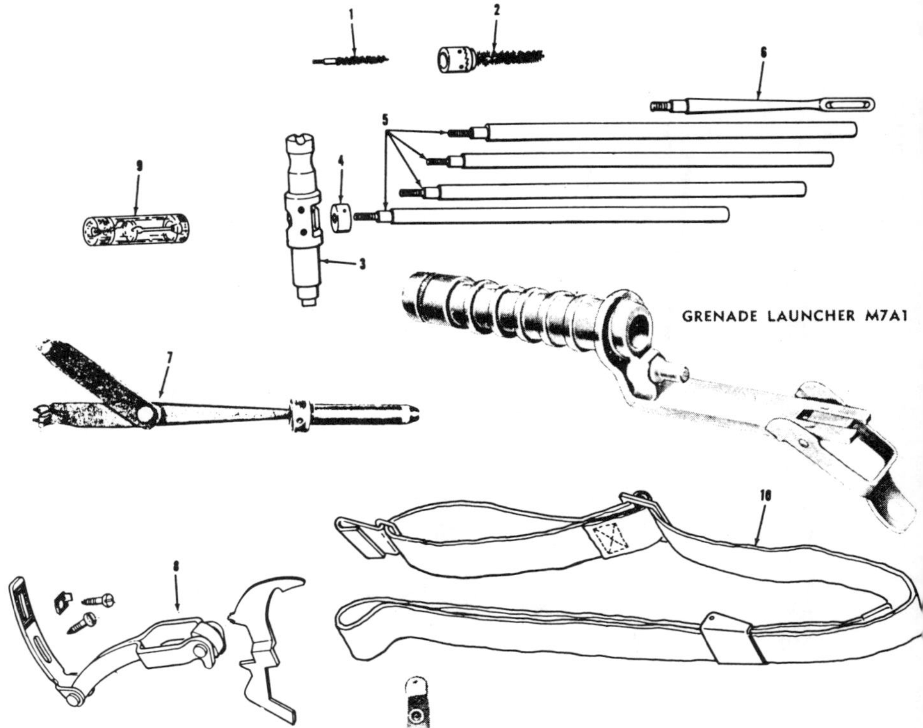

GRENADE LAUNCHER M7A1

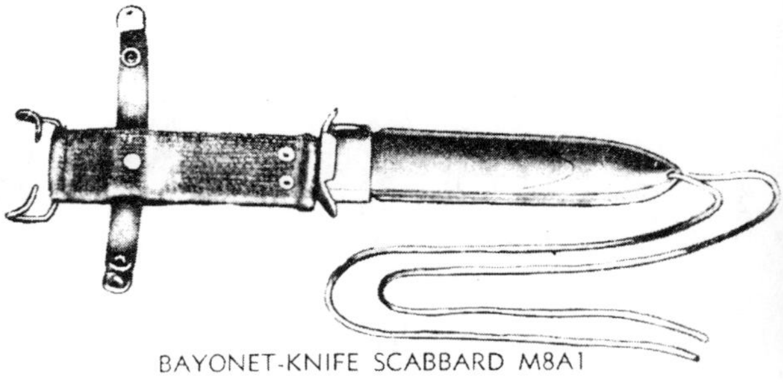

BAYONET-KNIFE SCABBARD M8A1

BAYONET-KNIFE M5

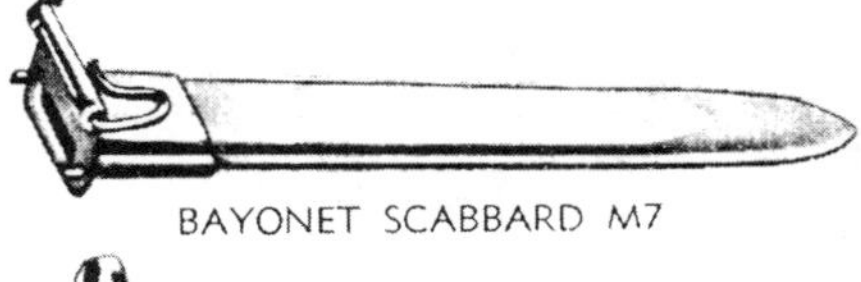

BAYONET SCABBARD M7

BAYONET M1

Sling, M1 - webbing (10)
Sling, M1907 - leather
Cleaning rod, jointed,
M10 (3-6)
Combination tool (7)
Chamber brush (2)
Oiler(9)
Winter trigger kit (8)
Bayonet M1
Bayonet- knife M5
Scabbard M7
Scabbard M8A1
Grenade Launchers M7,
M7A1, M7A2, M7A3
Sight, grenade launcher, M15

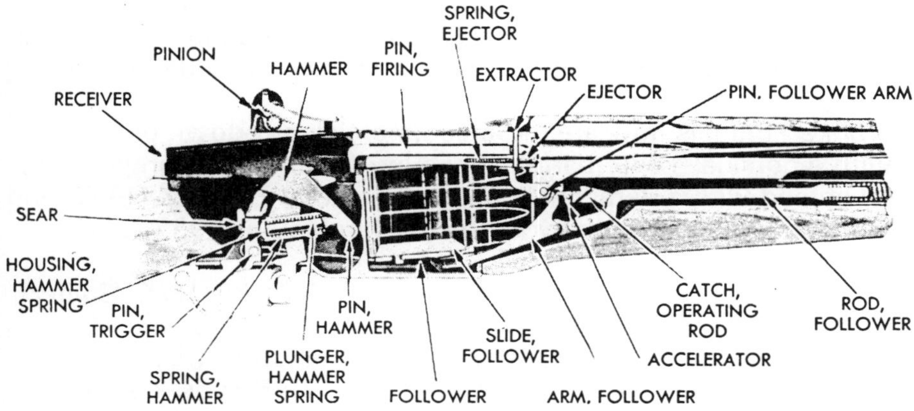

.30 M1 Garand action cut-away

John C. Garand was a Canadian who went to work at Springfield Armory in 1919 and finally retired from the factory in 1953. The U.S. Ordnance Dept. asked Garand to design a gas-actuated piston cylinder self-loader in 1926 which resulted in the .276 Garand; it was first tested in the fall of 1929.

.30 caliber versions were completed early in the 1930s and the Springfield Armory built 80 such rifles for trials in 1932. The U.S. Rifle Cal. .30 M1 was adopted on 9th January 1936, more colloquially known today as the 'Garand'. The first production .30 M1 was proofed on 21st July 1937 at Springfield Armory.

In 1940, the gas system was changed to a port rather than a trap design, which resulted in a .6-in. longer barrel and modified gas cylinder near the muzzle. Winchester Repeating Arms also made the wartime Garand and minor alterations were applied to the rearsight assembly and mode of production of some parts.

Two sniper variants were introduced during WW2, the M1C with its scope mounted on the receiver and the M1D which was mounted on the barrel. The telescope is necessarily offset due to the charger clip facility at the top of the action.

The Korean War saw the M1 Garand rifle back in production again with two new contractors, International Harvester and Harrington & Richardson Arms Co., along with various other sub-contractors also producing specific component parts.

The National Match model is the most refined M1, being set up at Springfield from mid-1953, initially for use at the Camp Perry matches. Springfield's Production of the NM model ceased in 1956 with a likely run of over 21,000 new production to which is added a similar number of rebuilds, many being FTR'd originals.

'Tanker' models now are more commercial, cut-down patterns with a nominal 18-in. barrel. However, Garand's design was later revamped with a detachable box magazine in 7.62mm NATO and adopted by the U.S. Army as the M14 in May of 1957.

	US Rifle M1	*US Rifle M1C (Sniper)*
Cartridge:	.30 M2 ball, tracer, &c.	.30 M2 ball
Muzzle velocity:	2,805 ft./sec.	2,805 ft./sec.
Maximum range:	3,450 yds. approx.	3,450 yds. approx.
Length OA:	43.6 in. (1107mm)	46.06 in. (1170mm) with T37 flash hider
Barrel length:	24.0 ins. (610mm)	24.0 ins. (610mm)
Barrel rifling:	4 groove, RH twist	4 groove, RH twist
Sight type:	Rear aperture, windage	Telescope M84
Sighted:	100 - 1,000 yds.	to 1,000 yds.
Sight radius:	27.9 ins. (708mm)	5-in. relief, 2.2 power
Operation:	Gas operated, rotating bolt, self-loading	Gas operated, rotating bolt, self-loading
Magazine:	Integral w/ 8-rd. clip	Integral w/ 8-rd. clip
Weights–empty:	9 lb. 7 ozs.	11 lb. 11 ozs.
loaded:	9 lb. 12 ozs.	12 lb. 1 oz.
clip, empty:	0 lb. 1 oz.	0 lb. 1 oz.
clip, charged:	0 lb. 5 ozs.	0 lb. 5 ozs.
w/ byt & sling:	11 lb. 6 ozs.	11 lb. 12 ozs. (no byt.)
Trigger pull:	4.5 - 7.5 lbs.	4.5 - 6.5 lbs.
Production:	1937-1956	1944-1945
Manufacturers:	Springfield Armory Winchester International Harvester Harrington & Richardson	Ordnance Dept.
Av. mfg. cost:	$26.00 in 1945	

Bayonet M1–	
length OA:	14.4 in. (365mm)
blade:	10.0 in. (254mm)
Bayonet M1905–	
length OA:	20.6 in. (523mm)
blade:	16.2 in. (411mm)